Alternatives

New Approaches to Traditional Christian Beliefs

William L. Fischer

unity®
HOUSE

Unity Village, Missouri

The stained-glass windows featured on the cover are from the Unity Temple on the Plaza, Kansas City, Missouri. The windows were conceived by Ernest Wilson, then minister of the Temple, and designed by noted Kansas City artist Paul Mann. The actual creation of the windows was completed by the Hopcroft Stained Glass Studios in 1971. Unity Temple is the home of the founding congregation of Unity.

Revised paperback edition 1994

Tenth printing 2007

Cover design by Tom Hubbard
Cover photography by Gene King

Library of Congress Catalog Card Number: 79-67005
ISBN 0-87159-283-5
ISBN 978-0-87159-283-5
Canada BN 13252 9033 RT

For Lucille—

wife of nearly half a century and
an epitome of love and devotion

Contents

Preface to the 1994 Edition

Throughout most of my life, I have had a keen interest in the religions of the world. I was born into and raised in a strict Protestant Christian denomination. Much of what I was taught left no room whatsoever for interpretation. I have always found this to be confining in my attempts to understand what the great religions of the world are trying to say and, especially, what the true message of Christianity is all about.

There came a time in my life when I was freed from the concept that there is only one meaning to any doctrinal point. This change in my thought left me free for spiritual exploration. I found that, with this exploration, several things happened to my belief system. Some of my childhood beliefs became strengthened, for they were valid from the beginning. But in many others, I found that there were alternate paths to walk along in my pursuit of greater spiritual understanding.

I have found that these alternatives had been revealed to me in three different ways. First of all, there was *observation*. I looked about myself and gained new insights into the nature of creation. I realize that the creation is not really complete, but we are still involved in what might be termed the "unending Genesis."

The second way in which I arrived at these alternatives was through *lucubration*. This is an old word that simply means to study by artificial light. In other words, some alternatives were revealed through research.

Most important, however, was the third method, which was *inspiration*. What came to me was revealed by the very Spirit of God within me. Obviously, I had to understand what Spirit was saying to me, and I did this to the best of my ability. This is the process Jesus mentioned when He said, "The Holy Spirit, whom the Father will send in my name, will teach you everything, and remind you of all that I have said to you" (Jn. 14:26 NRSV). This process of inner revelation has been the most exciting of the three.

As you now approach the remaining pages in this book, do so with an open mind. Exciting new concepts may be revealed to you, or you may stand even more firm in the beliefs that have sustained you so far in your life. Either way, you will be stronger in the experience.

If growth is promoted, bear in mind that growth means change, and change is not always comfortable. But the experience of personal growth is well worth temporary discomfort. I trust that what you are about to read will become an adventure in growth for you.

William L. Fischer
Lee's Summit, Missouri
April 1993

Foreword

Many of the doctrines and teachings of the Christian religion are accepted by its followers without question. Many of us learned the tenets of our religion early in life—perhaps during our Sunday school days. As life became more complicated, we simply continued to accept what we had learned earlier. Life no longer afforded time for religious exploration and development.

This book is intended to give you an opportunity to explore some of the beliefs you have accepted and to determine for yourself whether they are still fitting. In this exploration, several things may happen for you: You may become strengthened in your childhood beliefs; you may find, upon investigation, that the validity of some of your past beliefs is in question; or you may find there are alternative beliefs that make more sense to you today. In the pages ahead, such alternatives will be offered for your consideration.

Some people do not realize that certain points that have become Christian doctrine did so under great controversy. Their validity was questioned at the time they were adopted by the Church Fathers. For this reason, it seems that personal re-examination is in order.

No effort has been made here to separate you from cherished beliefs that are helpful in your life. Rather, this is an offering of alternatives to traditional concepts, an offering designed to enrich your life even more.

If you find that some of your beliefs are challenged, it can feel as if you yourself are being challenged. This is sometimes a painful process; but if growth results, it is also most rewarding. May the pages ahead represent an adventure for you!

God

$\mathcal{M}$ost of us, from our earliest learning experiences, have been taught that God is a supreme "man." We have been told that "God created man in his own image" (Gen. 1:27), and we have not realized that this image is male and female. Not fully understanding our own origin, we have easily decided to create God in man's image.

Consequently, we have made of God a "superman." Inasmuch as God has been around since the beginning of time, "He" would naturally have to be a very old man; so, we have given "Him" a flowing beard. Since the Judeo-Christian concept of God came out of a patriarchal (male-dominated) society, we have learned to always refer to God with male pronouns: He, Him, His.

Our teaching further told us that the abode of God is the kingdom of heaven. When we speak of heaven, we think of it as being "up." Therefore, we have assumed that heaven is in the sky, that perhaps God dwells somewhere on the periphery of our universe.

Some early cultures were multigod oriented. These gods were usually made visible through carved or sculpted "idols," and they often were related to everyday living. Some societies worshiped the elements of nature as their gods. Elaborate rituals were established in order to appease these gods and, consequently, to control the elements. Other societies worshiped female deities, undoubtedly because of woman's ability to give birth, which was tremendously awe-inspiring to primitive people. The worship of these gods and goddesses became the way of "pagans" with the advent of the one Hebrew God, Father of all.

There are places on this earth where it is thought that God can be contacted more easily and more readily than others. These have been designated as "sacred" places, and shrines have been built on many of them. Many persons have made long and difficult pilgrimages to such places in an effort to find and draw near to the presence of God.

All in all, we have made God most inaccessible. We have made "Him" into a "Man" with human attitudes and emotions magnified to supernatural proportions. We have placed the kingdom of God so far away that we do not really know how to "get there." We have made of God one whose love is to be greatly desired and whose wrath is to be feared. We have given God a whimsical personality: sometimes "He" answers our prayers and sometimes "He" does not. We have made God one who seems most pleased when we come to "Him" as praying beggars and sinners.

Can this truly be God . . . the God of all creation? Can this be the God who spoke to the heart of Jesus Christ and said, "This is my beloved Son, with whom I am well pleased" (Mt. 3:17)? Can this be the God, represented by Jesus Christ, who healed the minds and bodies of people, who provided them with food when they were hungry, and who has blessed and inspired so many people down through the centuries? Can this be the God who said, "Before they call I will answer" (Is. 65:24)?

Perhaps we need to take a look at this concept of God, to determine if this is really the God we worship. Is there an alternative to this concept, one that we can relate to in our daily life, in a contemporary sense? I believe there is.

When Jesus Christ spoke of God, He did not speak of a distant God; He said, "The Father is in me" (Jn.

10:38). Could God be any closer than that? If God was in Jesus Christ, is this same God in all persons? The argument against believing that God indwells each of us is that Jesus Christ was singled out by God for a special spiritual destiny. And so He was.

Still, the Bible clearly states that in the beginning God created all people—"man, male and female"—in the divine image and likeness. It is also written, "God saw everything that he had made, and behold, it was very good" (Gen. 1:31). In Genesis, we learn two very important things: God created us in the likeness of divinity and pronounced that creation good.

The Spirit, the breath of God, is in us. We do not have to put in a long-distance call to God every time we pray. We are not called upon to make long pilgrimages to sacred places. God is within us, completely accessible to us. We may contact God by turning quietly within ourselves. This is what Jesus Christ meant when He said, "But when you pray, go into your room and shut the door and pray to your Father who is in secret; and your Father who sees in secret will reward you" (Mt. 6:6).

Since this is what Jesus Christ taught about God, it is difficult to understand how Christians have taken an indwelling Spirit of goodness and shaped it into a supreme "Man" in a distant kingdom.

Does this mean that God is found *only* within people? Not at all. As Creator, God is imbued in all creation. The presence of God is not limited to people, but the presence of God finds aware and refined expression through people. "God slumbers in the rocks. God stirs in the flowers. God awakens in Man." The mountains reflect the majesty of God. A calm lake carries the message of the serenity of God. A sleeping infant reminds us of the uniqueness of God. The flaming red of a full-blown rose tells us of the beauty of God.

We could well say that God is where we find God. God is the principle responsible for all creation. The Principle cannot abandon the creation, without the creation ceasing to be. So, truly, God is in all things. There is no situation or thing on earth so mundane that it does not bear witness to the presence of God. There is no darkness so dark that the light of understanding cannot shine in it. There is no experience so critical that an activity of this all-pervading Spirit cannot harmonize it.

This, then, is your alternative: Instead of a distant, inaccessible, hard-to-please God, the God really represented by Jesus Christ is a God of healing and prosperity—an accommodating God, a God for whom no task is either too large or too small, a God who is "nearer than hands and feet, closer than breathing." This God is not a temperamental old man, but an indwelling Spirit, ever eager to find expression through creation—through you.

Jesus Christ

*T*raditionally, Jesus has been seen chiefly as a figure to be worshiped. Although no one can say for sure what He looked like, this has not inhibited sculptors and painters from trying to depict His image, nor have writers been stopped from creating many word pictures of Him.

Many of the great churches of the world have paintings and/or statues of Jesus, and there are people who go to these representations to pray. We have made of Jesus Christ a god, to be known only in awe and reverence. But He did not want this: "Why do you ask me about what is good? One there is who is good" (Mt. 19:17). At no time did He tell His followers to worship Him; instead, He gave that ringing command, "Follow me."

Still, we are awed by what He did for mankind. Jesus Christ showed all of us that we each have direct access to God. He did not walk across the land, saying, "Look what I, as the Son of God, can do." Rather, He walked among the people, telling them, in effect, "Here is what you, as a child of God, can do." At one point He even said, "Is it not written in your law, 'I said, you are gods'?" (Jn. 10:34) He told us of our true estate: we are reflections of God Almighty.

But it has been difficult for us to grasp such a lofty concept, for we have been taught by others that only Jesus was the offspring of God. It was He who healed "every disease and every infirmity." It was He who raised Lazarus from the dead. It was He who multiplied the loaves and fishes. It was He who told parables that have lived for ages. It was He who was resurrected from the dead. We may ask, "Can any other person do such things?"

The answer, according to Jesus, is yes. Even if no one has yet done them, we can, for Jesus said, "He who believes in me will also do the works that I do; and greater works than these will he do" (Jn. 14:12). Jesus believed that we could do such things. The problem is that we don't believe. Belief that we *can* perform miracles is the key factor in the doing.

Up until now we have worshiped and adored Jesus Christ, even though there is biblical evidence that He was not at all comfortable with this response to His teachings. What is our alternative? If we are not only to worship Jesus Christ, then how shall we regard Him? Why not do what He asked us to do—follow Him? His greatest role was that of Way-Shower.

A mystic is a person who believes that he or she has direct access to God. In this respect, Jesus Christ was a total mystic. But He wanted all of us to understand that we too are mystics. He wanted us to know that if we follow His teachings, we will also work the works of God.

In order to do this, we need to go back to the direct teachings of Jesus. We must not permit ourselves to become overly concerned with what either the church or its leaders have said about Him. The important thing is what Jesus Himself taught. We have become more concerned with the religion *about* Jesus Christ than with the religion *of* Jesus Christ.

How do we know how to follow Him? The answers are simple; activating the answers in our lives will be more difficult. We need only go to the Gospel accounts of His life, study them carefully, and make a sincere attempt to activate them in our own lives and affairs. This is our great alternative.

What are some of the general tenets of His teachings? What would be life-changing for us to follow?

The idea of *healing* was central to Jesus' ministry. The Bible records that He healed "all manner of disease." Nothing is incurable in the sight of God; therefore, nothing was incurable in the healing ministry of Jesus Christ. If we believe that we can do the works that He did, nothing shall be incurable to us, for we too will be working in the flow of the power of God. Therefore, one of our alternatives is to believe that, when we pray believing, there is an activity of healing working through us. We have the divine right to be well and strong, according to the example of Jesus Christ.

The idea of *love* was uppermost in Jesus' teachings. His example shows us that His love was so great that it embraced even His enemies. He instructed us to love our enemies and to pray for those who persecute us. If we are to exercise our alternative and really follow Him, our lives must be dominated by love. There would then be no room in our minds and hearts for thoughts and feelings of anything less than love—no hate, no envy, no jealousy, no malice. This may be the most important alternative that we follow: to be completely motivated with compassion. This makes of us radiating centers of divine love. As such, we make our greatest contribution to the world. When the time comes that the world is dominated by love, war shall be impossible. Many of the problems that confront the people of the world today will dissolve before the intense warmth of God's love, a love that finds expression through God's people.

The idea of *faith* was also exemplified by Jesus Christ. He referred to faith as the mountain-mover in our lives.

He taught that when people have sufficient faith, there is no problem in life that cannot be overcome. He conquered even death, through His faith in eternal life. As our Way-Shower, He demonstrated to us that we cannot live without faith. As we take up the quality of faith as a hallmark for our own lives, we find that we have the key to more abundant living. Faith has been referred to as a "key" to open life's doors. It truly is! A divinely inspired faith gives the vision and strength to scale the waiting hills of life and to know the exaltation of living at the peak of human capabilities.

Obviously the teachings of Jesus are intricate and extensive. But if you will take the time to delve deeply into those teachings, you will find that they are totally applicable to contemporary living. If, in addition to whatever feelings of awe and reverence you have toward Jesus, you will also seek to *follow* His teachings, you will find this experience a life-changing one.

Remember: Your alternative is to *follow* in His steps and to do so with an open mind and a sincere heart.

Humankind

*O*ne of the prominent beliefs concerning humankind is that we were "conceived in iniquity and born in sin." We have accepted this thinking of ourselves as incurable sinners, so much accepted it that it is a difficult exercise to entertain an alternative to this idea.

We have accepted, even concluded, that we are indelibly tainted with the original sin of Adam and Eve. But if we take the time to explore the Bible in depth, we will realize that the story of Adam and Eve is allegorical. It was composed after much of the rest of the Old Testament was recorded, designed to give a beginning to the story of human beings. We cannot deny that the story of creation is beautifully written, but we would do well to remind ourselves that it is a *human* endeavor to write of our beginnings.

Many of us have been bombarded since childhood with the teaching that we are miserable sinners, resulting from the "fall of Adam," and the implication has been that an entire lifetime would not be sufficient time to eradicate the taint of our sinfulness.

Is this our true estate? Are we doomed to spend our lifetime struggling to overcome the sin that we brought into this world at birth? Do we need to keep reminding ourselves (and God) of this sinfulness? Are there truly unforgivable sins? If we truly believed any of this, it would indeed seem that we were doomed. How can we ever surmount a burden of sin that is imposed upon us by the nature of our creation?

St. Paul shared this insight, teaching that we are "children of God, and if children, then heirs, heirs of God and fellow heirs with Christ" (Rom. 8:16-17). What a glorious insight into the nature of humanity!

The ancient Hebrew King David also had such an

insight; in Psalms 8:4-6, we read:

> "What is man that thou art mindful of him,
>   and the son of man that thou dost care for him?
> Yet thou hast made him little less than God,
>   and dost crown him with glory and honor.
> Thou hast given him dominion over the works of
>   thy hands;
>   thou hast put all things under his feet."

It is true that we have the right to take this alternative view of ourselves. The Bible is replete with references to the spiritual greatness of human beings. In our human inclination, we have tended to see ourselves as we appear to be, rather than as the true spiritual masterpieces we are.

But the time has come to change all that, for us to begin to appreciate the nature of our creation. The time has come for us to set aside the old and negative opinions we have accepted of ourselves and others. Yes, the time has come to appreciate the glory of our true estate. We really have been/are created in the image and likeness of God! There is a divine light that glows within each of us.

Jesus told us that we ought not to hide our light under a bushel. Rather, we should set it in a high place for all the world to see. That is our divine destiny—to be a light unto the world. The knowledge of this destiny is the viable alternative to thinking of ourselves as miserable sinners. "Let your light so shine" (Mt. 5:16). Accept this challenge, and let your light of divinity show all people that not only are you a true child of God, but they are too.

In a moment of great inspiration, William Shakespeare wrote: "What a piece of work is man! How noble in reason! How infinite in faculties! In form and moving, how express and admirable! In action, how like an angel! In apprehension, how like a god!"

Do you feel this way about yourself? Surely this is how God feels about you. We all need God in our lives, but we also must know that God needs us. How will God refine expression on earth if not through people—male and female? We are vehicles through which God is able to express and be conscious on earth. Can you accept the responsibility for this thinking? If you can and will, magnificent qualities will find expression through you. Your life will be changed into a glorious expression of exciting goodness. It is not a kind of goodness that will inhibit you, but one that will expand you. You will begin to feel the real possibilities of life.

There is also the thought that God blesses some people more than others, that God plays favorites. We look around us and see others who seem to be more favorably endowed than we are. If we have this feeling, we need to recall the important Bible passage: "God shows no partiality" (Rom. 2:11). This means that God looks upon all of us with an equal eye. Some persons take advantage of their divinity more than others, and we are inclined to envy them; but we must not. We need not be concerned with them. Remember Jesus' words: "What is that to you? Follow me!" (Jn. 21:22) Therefore, we must be about the business of acknowledging and expressing our own divinity.

When we do this, then we too are "about our Father's business," giving expression to the divine qualities with which each of us has been endowed.

Yes, this is our alternative: Rather than allow ourselves to be mired in the concept of original sin, we can see ourselves as we really are. We are God's children. Our souls are alight with the fire of heavenly virtues.

Prayer

*T*he most commonly used type of prayer is the prayer of supplication. We have somehow reached the conclusion that the only way we can have our prayers answered is to beg God. Consequently, we have devised prayers that confess to God our unworthiness to receive, and then we beg for the answer to be given to us anyway. This method of prayer is confusing.

It seems that we have concluded that we must fill the role of a praying beggar, that we must always come to God with our "hats in our hands," asking God to give us something that we do not have.

Some prayers are prayers of agony. There are times when we are in despair and desperately need divine intervention in our lives. The unfortunate thing about prayers of agony is that they are often not prayers at all—they are periods of concentrated worry, times when we give to God a recitation of our troubles. At no time during such a prayer do we demonstrate the openness and receptivity necessary for us to detect an answer, which is always positive.

Other prayers are perfunctory. On some occasions, to pray seems like the thing to do, so we pray. There is no real "heart" in our effort. This type of "praying" is sometimes done during a formal church service when we come to the point where the order of service calls for prayer, so we go through the motions of prayer. This is hardly conducive to real results.

Then there are the prayers that are read. They are usually "stock" prayers, written in a prayer book, a pamphlet, or some other kind of formal leaflet. We read those prayers because they seem to have the right words in them. These are often written by professional prayer composers and are beautiful indeed. But because they are someone else's prayers, they often lack the feeling that comes from praying from the heart.

Next, there are prayers that are said—some people "say" a prayer and others "pray" a prayer. Obviously, it is more effective to pray our prayers. Real prayer is an entrance into spiritual communion with God. This can only be done when we pray our own heartfelt prayers, when we pray in order to feel a sense of kinship with God and to know the supreme Power who is eager to give us all that is for our highest good.

The Apostle Paul instructed us to "pray constantly." How is this possible? We must go about our daily chores; we must earn our livings and live our lives. Certainly we cannot spend all our time in the formal act of praying.

This is where the alternative comes in: it is possible to pray without ceasing. This kind of praying is not done on our knees or with folded hands; the position of the body is unimportant. But the position of the mind is all important. We can have a constant *attitude* of prayer. Perhaps that sounds difficult, if not impossible; but once you understand what a prayerful attitude is, it will not only be possible to attain but highly practical.

To begin with, you will need to ask yourself some questions: Do you appreciate the possibilities of life? Do you want to be of help to your friends—even to people you hardly know? Do you want to have a better quality of life? Do you want to have the ability to think so clearly that you can evolve solutions to all of life's problems? If you can answer "yes" to these questions, then prayer without ceasing will come easily for you, even though you must practice an attitude of prayer in order to become adept.

Ralph Waldo Emerson once defined prayer as "the contemplation of the facts of life from the highest point of view." Applying this definition of prayer to our own lives, we can see that praying without ceasing is, in effect, keeping positive. It is no more than a simple but constant appreciation of life. Life has so many possibilities for us; those possibilities become personal experiences when we have conditioned our minds with appreciation. The mind then becomes similar to fertile soil into which good seeds (divine ideas) fall—to germinate, grow, and blossom into personal virtues.

Do not allow yourself to look at life from a valley. Lift up your thoughts and contemplate life from the highest point of view. From the high plateau of positive thinking, you are able to see life whole—with all its infinite possibilities. If you keep the high watch on your attitudes, you will be praying without ceasing and reaping the rewards.

To take your mind off yourself and pray for others will help in this process. There are two ways you can pray for others: you can use the "arms" or the "wings" of prayer. When you use the arms of prayer, you embrace someone in particular, by thinking of him or her specifically in the highest way you are capable of doing. He or she is the specific target of your prayers and is thus taken into the arms of prayer.

When you use the wings of prayer, you simply send your prayers forth to all who are receptive to them. These are great, sweeping prayers, sent winging on their way to do the general good.

Then, there is the passage in The Book of Job that says, "You will decide on a matter, and it will be established for you" (Job 22:28). This is the prayer of a positive mind. It is not a prayer beseeching God to hear; God already hears. This is a prayer of affirming good and accepting it with a grateful, confident heart.

As you condition your mind for receiving answers to prayers, be sure that you make an earnest effort to remove any mental debris you may have been collecting. A mind that is cluttered with negative thoughts cannot be receptive to divine answers. After your mental housecleaning, affirm the things you desire for yourself and for others; then be sure to spend some time in quiet listening. Too many people think that prayer is a monologue; this is not so. Prayer is a dialogue. After you have "let your requests be made known to God," it is important that you spend time in silence, for receiving. The voice of God has been called the "still small voice." To hear it requires hushed expectancy. Give God an opportunity to take part in this prayer dialogue.

The alternatives here are several. Each of them affords you an opportunity to draw closer in consciousness to God. When you are close in consciousness to God, you have a new self-appreciation; you are more assured, more considerate of others, and more Christlike in your actions. There is a special glow about those who are close to God; this is because you are special.

Worship

*W*hat is more prominent in the Christian world than the worship service? People who have no other association whatever with a church attend worship services on Sunday. Sunday has been set aside as a day of worship. It is the Sabbath, a day of resting from the work of the world. In the past many retail businesses were not allowed to be open on Sunday.

Most of us cannot deny, however, that we have sometimes gone to church on Sunday out of a sense of obligation. Even though we did not necessarily feel in a mood for worship, we attended church. When we have gone to church in this frame of mind, we have learned that it is not likely we will experience any great spiritual uplift. All of us have either had the experience of falling asleep in church or have observed another who did.

Perhaps we have gone to church out of a sense of responsibility to others—children in our family for whom we wanted to set a good "example"; a parent who insisted. We have learned that to enter into a worship service simply because of a sense of duty is hardly conducive to a major spiritual experience.

There are also persons—perhaps you have been one of them—who attend the Sunday worship service under a sense of duress. These are the persons who really do not want to attend, but do so because of the persuasion (often not gentle) of a loved one. A person attending church to make someone else happy is unlikely to get much out of the service itself, and he or she may even detract from the worship experience of others.

There are those of us who attend Sunday worship services simply so that we can be with other people.

Many lonely persons in the world have no social contacts other than through their churches. These are often older persons. Church attendance represents for them a respite from their loneliness, and it is obviously a beneficial practice. In many instances, the constructive social experience of attending church is a spiritual experience as well.

Other persons go to church for selfish reasons. I have known persons who were running for political office who went to church to solicit votes. Business people sometimes make business contacts before or after church services and attend strictly for that reason. I once knew a physician who told me he built up his medical practice through contacts he made in church. There are those who feel that being seen in church is just plain good for their community image. If political and business reasons are the only motivations for attending church, spiritual benefits can hardly be achieved.

Sometimes there are people who go to church just to get away from home. I have known persons who have gone to church simply to have an hour away from screaming children and/or a nagging spouse. These persons often do have a good spiritual experience at church, because they find the peace and harmony they have sought. However, if the desire is only to escape from something, rather than to enter into something spiritual, the benefits of a one-hour Sunday retreat will be limited.

Some persons don't go to church at all. Some of them completely ignore the worship experience in their lives. Others have private and intense worship experiences. Others "attend church" via television or radio.

Sunday-morning broadcast schedules on television and radio are filled with religious programs that originate from all parts of the country. Those who watch these programs can find them fulfilling if they truly enter into the spirit of worship.

And, of course, there are those who attend church and become mentally, emotionally, spiritually, and physically involved in the worship service. The sermon or lesson, the instructional part of the service, helps them to know how to live a more positive and productive life. The prayers or meditations, the experiential part of the service, enable them to feel the presence of God. This feeling can be carried over into everyday living and be of great value.

The dictionary says that to worship is "to feel extreme adoration or devotion." In this definition, the word *feel* is important. In the true worship experience, feeling is the essence. What you feel becomes a part of you; it builds into your nature. It is reflected in your life. It becomes a quality of your character. It is the light that shines through you.

The alternative here is not necessarily a substitute, but it could be. This is something you do in addition to your Sunday worship experience: it is worship on a daily basis. This worship occurs at any time and in any place that you feel adoration for and devotion to God.

This worship experience is not something that must be experienced in a church. Worship on a daily basis can be done at any place, any time. You may have a sacred and important place in your home—a place where you can become quiet and feel the presence of God. If this is the case, that place becomes your special altar, no matter how commonplace or ordinary it may appear to be.

Nature provides us with many inspiring and natural "altars." The things of nature often remind us of the attributes of God. We can look at a soaring mountain peak and think of it as a majestic altar. The calm waters of a placid lake can put us in the mood for worship. A quiet glen provides a gentle setting for worship. The places and times of worship are endless.

The important thing to remember is the alternative—that is, worship does not have to be limited to attending church, and it should not be. Letting your spirit soar in a sense of adoration and devotion to God should not be just a weekly experience. It can occur almost constantly. It could be called "practicing the presence of God." The quality of life derived from such experiences is indeed great beyond our wildest expectations.

The true worship experience will improve our lives, but it will not make of us "goody-goodies." Rather, it will cause us to be effervescent persons; persons with the magnetism to attract interesting friends into our lives; persons with a certain glow about us, which will make others want to be around us. Our minds will be filled with new, exciting ideas. Our bodies will be energized with the realization of God's life in them. Our hearts will brim with love, and we will live in a world of peace and harmony.

These are the benefits that will accrue when you exercise your alternative to worship constantly!

Baptism

*W*ater baptism has become an important part of the Christian practice. Some churches teach that there is no possibility of being "saved" unless baptism is experienced. There is controversy about how baptism should be administered. The religious groups that use immersion feel that anything less than total immersion is ineffective. In the architecture of these churches, the baptismal is a central and important part, usually featured in a prominent place. The immersionists also do baptisms in outdoor, natural settings—usually at a riverbank. The washing away of sins is believed to be accomplished with the symbolic total immersion.

The nonimmersionists sprinkle water onto those who are being baptized. They believe total immersion is unnecessary, reasoning that the actual act of baptism is symbolic and that the symbolism need not be carried to extremes.

This differentiation is so pronounced that in the military chaplaincy program there are two categories: immersionist and nonimmersionist.

Closely associated with baptism is the Christian concept of being born again. The born-again doctrine apparently originated with the nighttime encounter between Jesus and Nicodemus. Nicodemus came to Jesus and acknowledged that surely Jesus was a teacher who came from God. Jesus answered him, "Truly, truly, I say to you, unless one is born anew, he cannot see the kingdom of God" (Jn. 3:3).

The controversy lies within the question: What really constitutes being born again?

Nicodemus was totally baffled about the statement. He asked Jesus how this could be done. He wondered whether a man could "enter a second time into his

mother's womb and be born?" (Jn. 3:4). Spiritual re-
birth is still a matter of question.

There are churches that teach that an individual must
come to the altar, accept Jesus Christ as his or her
personal Savior, and be baptized (either by immersion
or sprinkling) in order to be born again. Other churches
teach that a profession of faith accomplishes the task.
Many churches do not emphasize the concept at all.

Because Jesus Christ Himself experienced water baptism at the hands of John the Baptist, many Christians
feel that it is a necessary part of the ultimate Christian
experience. Do you not, however, find it interesting to
note that after Jesus' experience with John, to the best
of our knowledge, He Himself never employed water
baptism for anyone else? From this, we must conclude
that He did not feel that this kind of baptism was necessary. Herein lies the baptism alternative.

In our consideration of this subject, we need to explore the method Jesus employed instead of water. The
Gospel of John gives insight. "Jesus said to them again,
'Peace be with you. As the Father has sent me, even so
I send you.' And when he had said this, he breathed on
them, and said to them, 'Receive the Holy Spirit' " (Jn.
20:21-22).

This has generally been accepted as the baptism of
Jesus' disciples. It is called spiritual or Holy Spirit baptism. This is the alternative:

Rather than being a ritual or ceremony formally en-
dorsed by the church and administered by it, baptism
can be understood as an intrinsically personal experience that occurs within us. In its deepest sense, baptism is a prayer experience with Spirit, an intimate dialogue between an individual and God.

There are two basic reasons for baptism. One is for the dedication of a life to spiritual ideals. This is the thought behind the baptism of children. The other reason is for cleansing or purification. With the adult, both of these purposes should be kept in mind during the prayer experience that results in spiritual baptism. As with all prayer, it is a mental process.

Let us first consider the idea of purification. This is what is implied in Jesus' comment that we need to be born of water. To be born of water is to remove from our consciousness the impurities of negation. We do this through the prayer-process called *denial.* Denial is the means by which we mentally, emotionally, and verbally refuse to allow anything that would impede our spiritual growth to remain in our minds. As long as such negation remains, we cannot have the spiritual experience of true baptism.

Jesus also spoke of the necessity of being born of the Spirit. This means that it is necessary to instill spiritual qualities into our consciousness to such an extent that they are automatically reflected in our lives. The way we do this is through the prayer process called *affirmation.* In affirmation, we declare for ourselves the establishment of great ideals. By a process known as the "law of mind action," when thoughts held in mind produce after their kind, these mind-ideals become qualities of character. Thus the change is effected in our lives.

This means that, whatever we were previously, we have become something new. In a real sense, we are born again. We are reborn into a new and heightened self, which is the objective of baptism and spiritual re-birth.

This becomes your alternative to consider concerning baptism: The baptism of water was that of John; Jesus' method was spiritual baptism. "For John baptized with water, but before many days you shall be baptized with the Holy Spirit. . . . You shall receive power when the Holy Spirit has come upon you" (Acts 1:5, 8).

Spiritual baptism, that of Jesus Christ, is a time of becoming very quiet within yourself and being at peace with God. Deny negation. Do not allow any of it to take residence in your mind. Affirm the Truth. Know that your mind is the habitat of productive goodness. Let your mind be filled with the beauty and glory of God's Spirit within you. Then you will be reborn into a new and exciting life.

Communion

*I*t would seem that the rite of Holy Communion (the Lord's Supper) is one of the most common doctrinal controversies in the church. How communion should be administered has long been a controversial issue. For centuries the church has been bickering about whether mixed or unmixed wine should be served, whether leavened or unleavened bread should be broken. There have been debates as to whether people should sit down, stand up, or kneel when partaking of the sacraments.

Then there are questions as to who should be admitted to the feast of Holy Communion and how often it should be prepared. In the Roman Catholic Church, infants were at one time permitted to partake and later forbidden. Since the ninth century the laity has received only the bread; the cup has been reserved for the priesthood. Only recently have there been some minor modifications in this practice.

In the Fourth Lateran Council, it was decreed that any believer should communicate at least one time each year, at Easter. Later it was determined that this sacrament should be received three times a year—Easter, Whitsuntide, and Christmas.

But perhaps the main controversies regard the nature of communion. One of these has been the authenticity of the theory of transubstantiation—that is, whether or not the bread and wine actually become the body and blood of Christ, as some churches say they do. In the Church of England, the archbishops were divided into three schools of thought. One school thought communion was a sacrifice of thanksgiving to God. Another thought that it was not a sacrifice, but a sacrificial feast. And the third of these said it was neither a sacrifice nor a sacrificial feast, but a simple commemoration. The Quakers have, in the last several hundred years, stopped observing the rite at all.

At the meeting of the World Council of Churches in Evanston, Illinois, in 1950, a committee was set up to study ways in which a common practice of partaking of communion could be established. This committee was to work on the problem and to report in ten years. At this writing, no acceptable plan has evolved.

With all this confusion about how Holy Communion should be observed and experienced, perhaps it is time to look at an alternative consideration. It is doubtful that Jesus intended to establish an institution for perpetual observance when He ate the Passover feast with His disciples. Communion, as it is commonly observed, is not a part of the religion of Jesus Christ; rather, it is part of the religion about Him.

We would do well to recall the words of the apostle Paul, "The kingdom of God is not food and drink but righteousness and peace and joy in the Holy Spirit" (Rom. 14:17).

The account of the Last Supper of Jesus and His disciples is given by all four Gospel writers. The Gospel According to Matthew records the words of Jesus Christ as He gave bread and wine to His disciples. But no expression implies that this feast was to be commemorated thereafter. In The Gospel According to Mark, the same words are recorded with still no intimation that the occasion was to be made into a ceremony. Luke, after relating the breaking of the bread, has these words, "Do this in remembrance of me." In John's gospel, although other occurrences of the same evening are related, this entire transaction is passed over without notice.

What did the expression "Do this in remembrance of

me" really signify? It was an affectionate expression. Jesus Christ was a Jew, sitting with His countrymen, observing their national feast. Perhaps He thought of His own impending crucifixion and wished to prepare the minds of His disciples for what was to come. In effect, this is what He said to them: "When hereafter you observe the Passover, it will have an altered aspect in your eyes. Think of me when, in the times to come, you observe the Passover together again."

On this occasion, Jesus was doing what the master of every household in Jerusalem was doing at the same hour. It was the custom for the master of the household to break the bread and bless it with the words, "Blessed be Thou, O Lord, our God, who gives us the fruit of the vine." Jesus did refer to His body and blood on this occasion, but they were not extraordinary expressions for Him. He always taught by parables and symbols; remember, He also said, "The flesh is of no avail; the words that I have spoken to you are spirit and life" (Jn. 6:63).

Now what about the alternative? Let's consider the sacraments, in a deep sense. Wine represents blood, and blood represents life. Therefore, wine is symbolic of the life of God coursing through our bodies. Bread represents the body of Christ, and this in turn is representative of divine substance. If the flesh profits nothing and the words are the important thing, why not observe communion by using our words in prayer? Since communion is concerned with the life and substance of God, then a real communion service is a prayer time when we appropriate more of divine life and substance in our lives.

This means that communion is a very personal thing; it does not necessarily have to be observed in a formal religious service. It can be done in the sanctity of our personal prayer place.

As you take time to have a real communion experience, you must become very still. In the dynamics of your silence, begin to think of the life and substance of God becoming more evident in every aspect of your life. Affirm for yourself that God's life is a powerful, divine element flowing through you, strengthening and energizing your body. God's life gives you a greater sense of service and a desire to be of greater benefit to others. In this rarefied consciousness of God working through you, you become more aware of His substance as evidenced in every aspect of your life. This substance represents more of everything in life that is for your highest good. Your life is mightily blessed.

You know that symbols are not necessary when you are capable of touching the presence of God within you without the use of them.

This is your alternative regarding communion: Instead of the formality of a religious rite, communion can be a spiritual experience privately conducted between you and your God. This is a life-changing experience.

What could be more inspiring?

Heaven

*W*hen I was a child, a most vivid description of heaven was given to me. I was told that if I was good I would go to heaven after I died. When I arrived I would be met at gates of pearl by none other than St. Peter himself. I would then be ushered to a personal audience with God. As near as I could determine, God would have an accounting sheet on me. He would carefully weigh the good things I had done against the bad. If the balance sheet was in my favor, I would gain admission into the kingdom of heaven.

Upon entering, I was told, I would be dazzled. The streets of heaven would be paved with gold. All the people would be angels. I was not told what all the angels would be doing to occupy themselves, other than harp-playing. Apparently, eternity would be spent either listening to or playing harp music.

I was also told that this kingdom was located somewhere in the sky. When I questioned where in the sky this location might be, no one could ever give me a clear answer. I was simply told that just as hell was "down," heaven was "up." This was my orientation concerning heaven. It was given to me not only in a serious manner, but as an absolute.

The thing that really bothered me about this was that the only way I could enjoy the ultimate ecstasy of God was by dying. I remember that I used to wish that there were some way to experience heaven without having to get old and die first. I even recall an old country-western song that said, in part, "Everybody wants to go to heaven, but nobody wants to die."

How did we human beings come into this concept of heaven? It is a concept built altogether upon the "fact" that heaven is above. We usually think that what is above is higher in dignity than what is beneath; therefore, heaven must be somewhere above us! It was natural that our thinking should go in this direction.

Also, we find it unbearable to think that life ends in a grave. That seems to be such an unfitting finish for a person, even though it is only the person's body that is buried. We want to think that some part of us lives on. We want to feel that the quality which we call life is so great that it cannot be limited to the relatively few years that most of us express on earth. We have a right to want to believe this.

But there is an alternative concept to the heaven traditionally taught, and this alternative is contained in the very words of Jesus Christ. Granted, it is written that when Jesus prayed, He lifted His eyes to heaven. But where did Jesus say heaven is located?

He was specific in this regard; He said, "The kingdom of heaven is at hand" (Mt. 4:17), and "The kingdom of God is in the midst of [within] you" (Lk. 17:21). This is an exciting concept. It means that heaven is here and now. It is not something to be experienced only after death of the body.

But if the kingdom of God is within us, what is it? The insight given to us by Charles Fillmore, co-founder of Unity School of Christianity, in the *Metaphysical Bible Dictionary* is this: "The kingdom of heaven, or of the heavens, is a state of consciousness in which the soul and body are in harmony with Divine Mind." This means that heaven is a state of consciousness in which we have so elevated our thoughts and feelings that they are in complete harmony with the Spirit of God within us. "Entering" the kingdom of heaven is an experience that any one of us can have here and now.

Note that I said "experience." Heaven is not a destination; it is an experience. But so often we are overly vague with such statements; let us be more specific.

If it is true (and it is) that we are created in the image and likeness of God, then the Spirit of God dwells within us. Where God dwells, there is heaven. Therefore, logic tells us that heaven is within us. The kingdom of heaven in us is the estate of perfect spiritual consciousness. It is that part of us where the supreme qualities of Spirit lie in waiting—waiting for us to allow them to find expression through us. These are the qualities of perfect love, peace, joy, health, courage, and all other expressions that represent the truly spiritual life. But these qualities are dormant until we consent to express them in our personal, spiritual character. How is this done?

It is accomplished through prayer. There is a specific technique that consists of denial—the removal of mental obstructions so that we may pray an effectual prayer—and the use of affirmation—to consciously establish divine qualities in our consciousness. In addition to the verbal aspects of our prayer, there is the matter of attitude.

One of the attitudes that must be removed is doubt. If there is even a shadow of doubt in our minds that any one of these divine qualities can well up within us and find expression through us, it is not likely that we will be elevated to a heavenly estate of consciousness. There must be total faith in order to have a total experience.

What then is the most important attitude to hold in order to lift our personal consciousness into a heavenly state? It is receptivity. We must be so receptive to the idea that God-qualities are coming to awareness in our personal consciousness that we find it impossible to harbor any doubt or fear to the contrary. Such an attitude may be called preparation of the individual consciousness for the advent of a personal experience of Spirit.

This spiritual experience is the sowing of the seed of divine ideas in the soil of our minds. Under the favorable climate of our attitude, these ideas germinate; then they sprout and come into fruition. The fruit of this process is experience. Since the seeds planted are love, peace, joy, health, courage, and so forth, experiences in keeping with these qualities come into our lives. We begin to give and receive truly spiritual qualities of life.

So the kingdom of heaven is at hand. It is yours to enjoy now! It is a truly heavenly experience to have divine qualities evidenced in your life. You do not have to wait until you die to know heaven. It is yours to know and experience now! This is what Jesus Christ wanted us to know.

Hell

$\mathcal{T}$he traditional concept of hell is a designated place where "bad" people go after they die. Most of us have been taught that if we would be "good," we would go to heaven, and if we didn't measure up to the standards of goodness, we would go to hell to spend our eternity in fiery punishment for failure.

It is fascinating to think how the fire-and-brimstone concept of hell might have evolved. The original Old Testament name for the place to which people went if they did not qualify for heaven is *Sheol.* But Sheol had no fire associated with it. Rather, it was shadowy and dim, owing to the absence of the Spirit of life. The terms *spirit* and *soul* are not used in connection with Sheol. Since we can also conclude that the body did not go to Sheol, it is difficult to know just what part of the person made this journey. In the original concept of Sheol, those who were there had no activity at all and could feel neither pain nor pleasure. Existence there was a dreamlike sort of thing.

Somewhere along the line of time, we became more descriptive about Sheol and changed its name to *hell.* Incredible, fiery descriptions of hell were preached, and the pain of the fiery existence was prominent. This teaching was inconsistent with the original concept of Sheol, the forerunner of hell.

The devil is the reigning monarch of the smokey kingdom of hell (see chapter on *Satan*). In our day Satan is pictured as being cunning and devious. The Old Testament writers made of him a sort of tempting, universal gay blade, who was always trying to get people into a pickle.

Since it has been known to mankind for a long time that the core of the earth is hot, to make this the location of hell seemed a natural thing to do. It is said that people "descend" into hell.

In the New Testament, the word *Gehenna* has been translated into hell. But this does not at all refer to the hell of traditional horror. Rather, it refers to the Valley of Hinnom; Ge Hinnom, it was called. This was a deep ravine near Jerusalem, which was used as a dumping ground for rubbish, garbage, and dead animals. To consume this refuse, a fire was kept burning at all times. Because this was the city incinerator and kept burning constantly, it was sometimes called the "eternal fire."

During the time of Jesus Christ, when the yoke of Roman occupation was heavy, it is said that some of the Jewish people took to human sacrifice. To do this, they converted to an ancient Semitic religion of the worship of Molech. Molech was the deity to whom children, preferably the firstborn, were sometimes offered by fire sacrifice.

Legend has it that a statue of Molech was placed at the crest of the hill over Gehenna. Children were placed on the arms of the statue, rolled off and down into the fire in the valley, where they were sacrificed. Jesus' reference to the hellfire was to this prohibited practice, not to an eternal damnation after death.

So, you see, the entire concept of a burning hell after death is something of nebulous content. There is no real basis for accepting this belief. It has served the church well, because it has been a fear tool for getting the followers of the church to abide by its mandates.

If the validity of the traditional concept of hell is in question, what is the alternative? It is that hell is not a destination. Rather, it is an experience of life. Who among us has not "been through hell" in some way or another? It has been appropriately said by Dr. James

Fischer that: "The tortures of hell are not in the core of the earth, but in the very core of life. Here, too, is heaven. And also that vast purgatory in between, populated by those who have found neither overwhelming torture, nor profound contempt—the lost souls ambling without purpose through their allotment of time."

Yes, hell is a state of consciousness. When we have permitted our thoughts and emotions to degenerate sufficiently, we suffer through experiences that seem to be degrading to our true, spiritual nature.

God has blessed us with divine purpose and presence, through the Spirit that indwells all of us. In this Spirit are all the qualities that comprise the true character of God. When we are expressing the antithesis of these qualities, our life becomes a living hell.

In the *Metaphysical Bible Dictionary*, Charles Fillmore states: "One does not have to die in order to go to hell, any more than one has to die to go to heaven. Both are states of mind, and conditions, which people experience as a direct outworking of their thoughts, beliefs, words, and acts. If one's mental processes are out of harmony with the law of man's [sic] being, they result in trouble and sorrow; mental as well as bodily anguish overtakes one, and this is hell."

We have all been taught that through our behavior we choose whether we shall experience heaven or hell. This is true, but this refers to now, not to some afterlife. It is a contemporary experience. If any one of us is going to experience hell, we can be sure that it will be during his or her earthly lifetime.

When the Old Testament writers referred to Sheol, it was to a grave rather than to an eternal destination. Likewise, when we experience hell now, it is as if we have buried ourselves with trouble. We have shut ourselves out from all the light and beauty that life is. Somehow, we have made the choice not to express the mystical qualities of God. This is to lie in the grave of negation.

It is our right to do this, since God has given us free will. But it is also our right not to. It is our right, through our divine heritage, to let ourselves be the free and open channels through which divine qualities of Spirit may express beauty. This is to refuse hell on earth. This is our great alternative.

> The mind is its own place, and in itself
> Can make a Heav'n of Hell, A Hell of Heav'n.
>
> —John Milton

> I sent my Soul through the Invisible,
> Some letter of that After-life to spell:
> And by and by my Soul returned to me,
> And answer'd, "I Myself am Heav'n and
>   Hell."
>
> —Omar Khayyam

Satan

$\mathcal{T}$he popular view of Satan is somewhat comical. He is caricatured as being small in stature, red in color, with small horns in his forehead, a pointed tail, and carrying a pitchfork, which is the weapon supposedly used to prod people into sinning. Sometimes he is pictured with a moustache and beard. He is also shown as having cloven hooves and very much resembling the mythical Greek god Pan.

Tremendous cunning and power are attributed to Satan by some people. It is said that sometimes a battle rages between Satan and God over the custody of a person's soul. The devil supposedly wins an occasional battle. This is a rather frightening consideration, because it accords more power to Satan than to God. It would make us wonder if we have a right to call God "Almighty." Perhaps, if this were the case, we would more appropriately call God "partly mighty."

In the Old Testament book of Job, there is an interesting story concerning Satan. Job is put to many trying tests to see whether he will remain loyal to God. Job's virtue prevails. The prominence of Satan in this fictional drama, however, seems to have given "him" a powerful place of consideration in the Judeo-Christian tradition. Thus it is that the traditional view of Satan is that of a second god, a god of evil who prevails in today's world to influence the evil-doing of humankind.

Where did the belief in Satan originate? In the purest Jewish tradition, there is only one God. This God created the earth and made it a garden, peopled this earth with all sorts of creatures, warmed it with the sun, enchanted it with the moon, and dazzled it with the stars.

The "satanic" influence came on the scene only when

God's people began to get their own ideas, which were not in keeping with the divine intentions of God. In the allegory of creation, there was no devil until Adam and Eve began to think in opposition to divine principles. This is important for us to remember.

We must also remember that the story of creation was not the first part of the Old Testament to be written. During the period in Jewish history known as the Babylonian captivity (nearly 600 years before the time of Jesus Christ), the first of the Jewish scriptures were recorded. Prior to this time, they were handed down from mouth to ear, from generation to generation, in what was called the oral tradition. The first Bible stories began with Abraham. It was later deemed desirable to write the story of creation.

What influenced the introduction of a satanic character into the allegory of creation? The actual origin of the concept of Satan is hidden in almost impenetrable mystery. But one tempting trail leads to the religion of the Persians. The ancient Persians had a two-god religion: one god was Ahriman, the god of darkness and evil; the other was Ormazd, the god of light and goodness. Many religious scholars feel that this Persian philosophy had an influence on Hebrew theology; hence, the character of Satan became a part of the Hebrew legends, and these legends, in turn, became the basis for the Hebrew scriptures.

Another promising trail leads to the Babylonian legend of the creation of the world. In this legend, there is a fallen angel named Kingu. He is said to have had an army of demons who went around helping people get into trouble. Some people feel that Isaiah's reference to Lucifer relates to this fallen angel; but Isaiah's reference is to Daystar, a name the Babylonian king used for himself.

Greek mythology also comes into the picture here. Hades was the kingdom of the dead, with both Elysian fields for the good and places of torment for the wicked. The mythical Greek gods were in charge of these places—the good gods were in charge of the good places and the bad gods in charge of the bad places. As already noted, the depiction of Satan in our time strongly resembles the Greek god Pan.

Because the Jews were in captivity in Babylon for about seventy years, it is likely that Babylonian legends would have influenced the Hebrew legends. Following the Babylonian captivity, there was the Persian occupation of Palestine, with the likely influence of Ahriman. This was followed by the Greek occupation and the possible and likely influence of Greek mythology. All this happened from about 600 B.C. to 120 B.C.—a formative period in Jewish religious thought. Satan makes a couple of other brief appearances in the books of Zechariah and Chronicles.

There is not much said about Satan in the New Testament. Paul makes one reference to the "devil" in 2 Corinthians 4:4: "The god of this world has blinded the minds of the unbelievers, to keep them from seeing the light of the gospel of the glory of Christ, who is the likeness of God."

It is written that a "tempter" came to Jesus. Though it is not written who this tempter was, Jesus later called "him" Satan. Jesus was in the wilderness and was tempted to change stones into bread. It is reasonable to assume that the tempter was the voice of human hunger speaking to Him. When He was at the pinnacle of the temple and was tempted to throw Himself off and land safely, it was probably the voice of a human desire for quick, sensational recognition. In the third temptation, He thought about becoming the political and military leader that the Jews expected their Messiah to be—and to worship materiality that would go with filling such a role. This was the voice of worldliness speaking to Him. There was no being outside Jesus, only the voice of His own human nature. For example, the pinnacle of the temple was a high platform where Roman soldiers had an outpost. If there had been a visible Satan there, these soldiers would have encountered "him" and attempted to destroy "him."

Each time Jesus Christ, in His higher nature, rejected the temptation. Had He succumbed, the power of God working through Him would have been nothing more nor less than magic to Him. But because He remained in a high state of spiritual consciousness, He became the ethical Messiah of the world.

Here, then, is the alternative concept of satan (which we deliberately do not capitalize since we are not referring to a separate being "out there"): Satan is not an impish being with a pitchfork, prodding people into a sinful life; rather, satan is the lower nature of all people. It is the self of us that can tempt us to do things that we know are not for our highest good. Within us, satan is the selfish, human, cunning, devious ego of limitation that motivates the human personality to turn away from God. It is the part of us that must decrease as our spiritual nature increases.

How do we overrule this part of us? "I, when I am lifted up from the earth, will draw all men to myself" (Jn. 12:32). We must elevate our desires of human appetite, raise the standards of our moral passions, bear up our spiritual aspirations, and be receptive to the drawing power of Christ. This is to lift up and spiritualize the human self, thus defeating our "satanic" nature. When this happens, the kingdom of Christlikeness will be established in our hearts, minds, and worlds. This is the great personal victory, which is the objective of true Christianity. Rather than doing battle with an external force that doesn't exist, the overruling of the lower nature by the higher is the ultimate accomplishment.

Sin

$\mathcal{M}$ost religions give a lot of attention to the subject of sin. This is because sin is degrading to the person and religion is designed to upgrade people. The way religion has used the concept of sin, however, is questionable. If religion has used the accusation that a person has sinned in order to make him or her feel more guilty and, therefore, more dependent on the church for salvation, this is indeed a questionable tactic. And if the church has taken a person's feeling of sinfulness and used this to make the person fearful of a burning hereafter, the ethic of this approach is also questionable.

When I was growing up, the sins that were applicable to me were not hard to define. First, I was taught that it was a sin not to empty my plate at dinnertime—because there were so many hungry people in the world. Next, I was not supposed to use swear words. And finally, my morals were to be above reproach. Basically, then, sin dealt with dinnertime, swearing, and sexual behavior.

The reference to eating everything on my plate was born out of natural parental concern for my physical well-being. To call it a sin when I did not clean my plate was nothing more nor less than a parental tactic, and understandable.

Taking the Lord's name in vain was another matter. Usually the curse words that were condemned came from the New Testament. To use the name of Jesus Christ, or any part of it, during an expression of anger or hostility is certainly immature. There is no question in my mind that such use of the Master's name is wrong. It also usually indicates a limited vocabulary on the part of the user.

But we must remember that the commandment—
"You shall not take the name of the Lord your God in
vain"—was given to us through the Old Testament (Ex.
20:7). What was the name of the Lord according to
Moses, who gave us this commandment? It certainly
was not Jesus Christ. God gave Moses the name during
the experience of the burning bush. You will recall that
Moses wanted to know whose voice it was who spoke to
him. That voice, the voice of God, identified as "I Am
Who I Am." When Moses wanted some authority for
returning to Egypt, this same Divine voice said, "Say
this to the people of Israel, 'I AM has sent me to you'"
(Ex. 3:14). Keep this in mind, because one of your
alternatives on the subject of sin lies within this infor-
mation.

The third area of sin dealt with moral behavior. If we
are inclined toward reckless promiscuity in our moral
behavior, it is often a symptom of a poor self-image. A
person who thinks well of himself or herself is not inclined toward this kind of behavior pattern. I do not
know if such behavior is a sin against God; but I am
sure that it is a sin against ourselves. If we truly believe
that we are spiritual beings, how is it possible to degrade ourselves through any behavior we deem as de-
meaning? So, in this area of sin, we need to take a
good look at how we really feel about ourselves and
our actions.

Traditionally, sin has been defined as a missing of
the mark. This means falling short of our highest potential. There are obviously many ways that we can and
do fall short. The important thing to remind ourselves
is that such falling short is not, does not have to be, a
permanent life experience. There is a definite remedy

for it.

Consider the quality of our words. As mentioned, the name of God as revealed to Moses is I AM. This means that anytime we use the words *I am* associated with any quality that would degrade or betray our spiritual character, we are taking the Lord's name in vain. Any time we say, "I am sick," or "I am poor," or "I am angry," we are associating the name of God with qualities that are the antithesis of the true character of God.

Herein lies our alternative. To use the words *I am* in this way is much more subtle profanity than the kind usually thought of as profane. Therefore, the ill effects of such an association can creep into our lives without our realizing what we have done to ourselves. Our words do have a tremendous effect upon our well-being. Therefore, it is important that we never associate the words *I am* with anything less than the qualities we normally associate with God. We need to affirm: *I am well and strong. I am alive with the joy of God. I am rich with God's bountiful supply.* This is to use the name of God as it was intended to be used.

There is also an alternative to be considered in the very definition of the word *sin*. We have most often thought of sin as a falling short of the mark. The degree of the sin has been determined by how far short of the mark we fell. Also, there was some question as to what the "mark" we aspire to reach really was.

The alternative definition of sin is "living under a false sense of separation from God." It is a false *sense* of separation because we cannot actually be separated from God. God is our very Spirit, the life that pulsates in and through our beings.

However, if we labor under the delusion that we are

separated from God, the effect is almost as if we were. If, in our own consciousness, we feel that God is "there" and we are "here," we will feel separated from our highest good. We will feel as if we really are poor, tired, sick, and the rest of that negative host.

For this reason, every prayer that we pray should be one for healing—to heal our sense of separation from God. It may well be that this sense of separateness is the only real sin. Everything we experience that could be termed sinful stems from this sense of separation from God.

If we feel at one with God, which we truly are, how could we ever feel deprived of any good thing in life? Much to the contrary, a feeling of at-one-ness with God gives us a sense of assurance that all is well with our world. We know that God is blessing us constantly with the strength of Divine Presence, which works mightily in and through us.

This was the great secret to the Messiahship of Jesus Christ. "I and the Father are one," He said. He meant for us to know this Truth for ourselves. When we do know this Truth, there can be no feeling of separation from God. Then the one major and basic sin is removed from our lives. When this falseness disappears from our thinking, fantastic things happen to us. Our minds become illumined with actual, useful wisdom. Divine energy flows through our bodies, revitalizing us. From our hearts the very love of God flows, as compassion toward all. Our personal worlds are peacefully prosperous, and we are grateful.

Give some serious thought to this alternative concept of sin. To feel at one with God is life's greatest feeling.

Life After Death

$\mathcal{B}$efore we begin to think about life after death, it is necessary to come to an understanding of the experience called "death." Death seems like such a final thing. In order to conform to the practices of our society, we find it necessary to make all the trying funeral arrangements, even though we may not agree with the practices involved in a contemporary funeral. There are visiting hours, the memorial service itself, and a trip to the cemetery. When the committal service at the cemetery is over, it all seems so final—we often even refer to the gravesite as the "final resting place." A life is over.

Is it? Is life over when we leave the body of a loved one at the cemetery? Obviously, the body is no longer alive. But is the body the *person* we loved? Hardly! We really loved that person's character, his or her responsive mind and loving heart and compassionate soul. These do not die. If nothing else, they live on in our memory. We are the ones who choose how long and how pleasant our memory of them shall be.

Life is the supreme quality of God. Without life, none of the other qualities could exist. The human body is fragile. Surely the God who created this life would not confine it to the limitations of this fragility. The actual quality of life itself is eternal. It has lived on through the ages and shall continue forever. This is the nature of life, as dictated by its history, its present, and its prognosis.

At the time of death, or soon after, the soul is believed to leave the body. This part of us that lives on is an unseen Self, spirituality with its own identity. But where does this invisible substance go? Traditionally, we have thought that it goes either to heaven or to hell, depending on the quality of personal behavior.

But let me give you an alternative—and please hear it through before you reject or accept it. It is reincarnation. This is the teaching that the "dead" person lives again as a human being in another human body. The teaching of reincarnation is not foreign to religious thought; it is enthusiastically embraced by many of the major world religions, especially the Eastern ones. It is not even foreign to Christianity. As a matter of fact, it was fairly well accepted in Christian thought until the Council of Constantinople in A.D. 533, when a ruling was made by the Church Fathers against it.

The question we are dealing with is simply this: Have we lived before in another body, and will we live again in another body after we leave this one?

Jesus Christ did not deal directly with reincarnation, but He did refer to it. It was a part of the teachings of the Essenes, a prominent sect of His day. There are some historians who believe that Jesus was an Essene in His thought, if not in fact. Reincarnation, it seems, was one of the accepted ideas of those times. Jesus opposed many of the teachings of the times, but we have no record that He ever repudiated or denied reincarnation.

There is an interesting observation recorded by Matthew in which Jesus referred to John the Baptist, saying, "I tell you that Elijah has already come" (Mt. 17:12), and again in Mark 9:11-13, we read: "And they asked him, 'Why do the scribes say that first Elijah must come?' And he said to them, 'Elijah does come first to restore all things . . . . I tell you that Elijah has come, and they did to him whatever they pleased, as it is written of him.'" It is generally accepted that Jesus was declaring that John the Baptist was one and the same as the reincarnation of Elijah.

In Matthew 16:13-14, we read that Jesus asked His disciples: " 'Who do men say that the Son of man is?' And they said, 'Some say John the Baptist, others say Elijah, and others Jeremiah or one of the prophets.'" From this statement, we may conclude that reincarnation was a common idea. Note that Jesus did not rebuke them for talking nonsense, nor did He condemn the idea. He went on to ask them not who the people said He was but who they, the disciples, said He was; and Simon Peter replied, "You are the Christ" (Mt. 16:16).

We cannot say that reincarnation is actually taught in the New Testament, but we can see that it was a current idea, which was neither denied nor criticized. When the early church, through the Council of Constantinople, rejected reincarnation, the teaching was discarded by a slim vote. However, even after official church rejection, the teaching was accepted by such notables as St. Augustine and St. Francis of Assisi.

There are exciting possibilities to think about in relation to reincarnation. For one thing, it means that we do not have just one physical lifetime in which to "qualify" for heaven. Rather, life is much like going to school, and each lifetime can be seen as a grade in our education. We learn the lessons we need to learn, then we move on to the next grade. Ultimately, we will graduate. That is, we will reach perfection. This may be what Jesus meant by saying, "You, therefore, must be perfect, as your heavenly Father is perfect" (Mt. 5:48). Perfection surely cannot be attained in one lifetime. It seems that in this one lifetime, we do not even know what perfection is.

Most persons do not fulfill their potential in a lifetime. But there is great hope in knowing that we shall have another chance, more opportunity than we can dream of. God is calling us all to perfection and intends for us to enjoy eternal life. Surely the loving God who created us does not demand that we accomplish all in one brief earthly experience. Even so, with God, all things are possible.

If you accept reincarnation as a viable alternative to what you have previously believed concerning life after death, you can get excited to know that this lifetime is preparation for the next. This gives incentive to grow through whatever challenges you are now encountering. If you learn the lesson of any challenge, you will never have to learn that lesson again—either in this "lifetime" or in one to come. This means that subsequent lifetimes will be easier, as you move toward that great and final objective—to be perfect, as your God in heaven is perfect.

Though a radical change from conventional thinking concerning life after death, reincarnation is possible and logical. This makes it an exciting alternative.

Conclusion

$\mathcal{T}$o accept an alternative to a belief that you have long held is not easy. Perhaps you have found it easy to accept some of these ideas but not others. If this is the case, fine. Accept those you can and set aside those you cannot. You can only discard old beliefs and accept new ones if it is possible for you to live with the new instead of the old.

After you have accepted what you can, set this book aside. Then at some future time, perhaps you will want to reread some of the chapters that contain ideas difficult at first to accept.

You may want to reject completely some of the alternatives stated here. That is your right and your responsibility to yourself. These are sincerely offered to you as possibilities for stretching your being, to stimulate you to think about what you may have been accepting without serious prayer and questioning.

Whatever it is that you believe about the subjects covered in this book, always bear in mind that life is a great adventure. Embark on this adventure with a stout heart and an expectant mind. If you are not happy with your life adventure, change it, make a new start, no matter where you are along life's way.

The God who made you can and will remake you, if you so choose. God smiles on you as a supreme creation, enfolding you in infinite love and wisdom—even though you make mistakes along the way to perfect understanding.

Happy living!

Further Reading

If you would like to learn more about the Unity alternative, the following books are recommended:

Christian Healing by Charles Fillmore

How to Let God Help You by Myrtle Fillmore

In the Flow of Life by Eric Butterworth

Lessons in Truth by H. Emilie Cady

The Quest and *Adventures on the Quest* (set)
  by Richard and Mary-Alice Jafolla

The Simple Truth by Mary-Alice and Richard Jafolla

The Story of Unity by James Dillet Freeman

Unity: A Quest for Truth by Eric Butterworth

To purchase any of these books, call your local Unity church or center or call the Customer Service Department at Unity Village, Missouri: 816-969-2069 or 1-800-669-0282.

About the Author

The Reverend William L. Fischer was a well-known leader in the Unity movement. He served as director of retreats at Unity School of Christianity, Unity Village, Missouri, for over thirteen years.

Born in Sharpsburg, Pennsylvania, in 1926, Reverend Fischer grew up with the Unity teachings and devoted his life to service in the Unity movement. Ordained a Unity minister in 1953, Bill served ministries in Kansas City, Missouri; Detroit, Michigan; Des Moines, Iowa; Delray Beach, Florida; and Akron, Ohio. For ten years, he directed Unity's ministerial training program. Prior to assuming his position as director of retreats, Bill directed Unity's Radio/Television Department and wrote the scripts for "The Word," which was aired nationally.

He is the author of two books published by Unity School: *The Master Craft of Living,* no longer in print, and *Alternatives.*

An articulate and dynamic speaker, Bill spoke throughout the United States, and in Germany, Switzerland, Japan, England, Canada, Puerto Rico, Trinidad, and Jamaica. His interest in biblical history led him to conduct five tours to the Holy Land. He also recorded the cassette album *The Angelic Consciousness.*

Bill Fischer was the first recipient of the Charles Fillmore Award, given to him because of his "visionary consciousness and dynamic leadership."

Reverend Fischer made his transition on June 27, 1994. He is survived by his wife Lucille and two grown children.

Printed in the U.S.A.

B0158-13918-5C-12-07 Q